YOUNG SCIENTISTS

The Body

Published by
Smart Apple Media
123 South Broad Street
Mankato, Minnesota 56001

Cover design by Patricia Bickner Linder
Interior design by Neil Sayer

Photographs by The Image Bank,
Robert Harding Picture Library,
Science Photo Library, Alan Towse

Printed in Hong Kong.

Library of Congress Cataloging-in-Publication Data

Dixon, Malcolm and Karen Smith.
The body / by Malcolm Dixon and Karen Smith.
p. cm. — (Young scientists)

Includes index.
Summary: Surveys the structure and function of various
parts of the human body, with simple activities to reinforce
the information given.
ISBN: 1-887068-69-4
1. Body, Human—Juvenile literature. 2. Human anatomy—
Juvenile literature. [1. Body, Human. 2. Human physiology.]
I. Smith, Karen, 1958- II. Title. III. Series: Dixon, Malcolm.
Young scientists.

QM27.D56   1999
612—dc21   98-6973

First edition

2 4 6 8 9 7 5 3 1

YOUNG SCIENTISTS

The Body

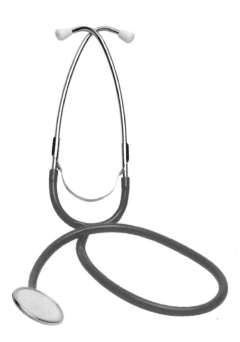

Malcolm Dixon
and Karen Smith

Smart Apple Media

NOTES FOR TEACHERS AND PARENTS

About you (pages 6-7)
It is important to discuss the meaning of words which may be new to the children, such as "similar," "similarities," and "differences." Try to develop an understanding of the massive scale of millions and billions. "Record" as used here could include drawing, writing, or using a tape recorder. Children are likely to know the word "weight," but "mass" is actually the correct scientific term.

Your skeleton (pages 8-9)
Show what would happen to our bodies without the support of a skeleton by getting a child to put a coat on and then remove it so that it drops to the floor. It would be useful to have a model skeleton and/or X-ray images to show and discuss the bones in the body. Point out that arms and legs have three bones, although only two can be felt.

On the move (pages 10-11)
The knee has a hinge joint; its backward and forward movement can be demonstrated and related to the elbow joint. Further discussion might involve the movement in many directions at the shoulders and hips. This is due to ball and socket joints. Muscles are attached to bones and cause the joints to move by contracting and relaxing.

Hands and feet (pages 12-13)
Children may have more difficulty in discussing similarities between hands and feet than they do in identifying differences. Our hands and feet do, in fact, have similar bone arrangements. The arches of our feet act like a shock-absorbing system as we walk or run.

Your heart (pages 14-15)
Discuss the meaning of the words "pump" and "pulse." Explain that arteries and veins enable blood to travel throughout the human body. Children may need help in finding their pulse and adjusting the position of the pulse-tester. Another, sometimes easier place to feel the pulse is on the neck, under the jaw bone. Discuss healthy diets and exercise as ways to keep the heart healthy.

Breathing (pages 16-17)
An extension activity would be to measure a child's chest measurement when breathing in and breathing out. The difference in the measurements gives the child's chest expansion. This could be compared to that of an adult.

Your amazing senses (pages 18-19)
Our sense organs are made of concentrations of cells which are sensitive to one kind of stimulus. One possibility for a smell test is to use containers, each with a different-scented substance (onion, perfume, etc).

Looking at eyes (pages 20-21)
You will need to talk about the pupil, the retina (a light-sensitive area inside the eye), and the meaning of "signals." The colored part of the eye—the iris—controls the amount of light entering the eye by contracting and relaxing, altering the size of the pupil.

Ears to hear (pages 22-23)
Discuss the meaning of "vibrate" and relate this to the children's observations of the drum and ruler. Talk about how these vibrations cause the air to vibrate and, in turn, cause movement within our ears. A further demonstration of vibrations could involve watching how a suspended ping-pong ball moves when placed against a tuning fork.

Your skin and hair (pages 24-25)
It may be helpful to demonstrate the idea of layers by using a suitable aid such as a layered cake. The hairs on our bodies provide a sort of human "fur." When fingerprinting, explain that every fingerprint in the world is different.

Your teeth (pages 26-27)
Baby teeth start to fall out at about six years of age. The incisors are used for cutting and slicing food, while the molars, which are broad and flat, are used for chewing and grinding. The different shapes of our teeth are related to their different purposes. Leaflets from a dentist will help in discussing the need for daily oral hygiene.

Growing and staying healthy (pages 28-29)
Discuss in a simple way how food is broken down as it passes through our bodies. Start by talking about how we chew food and mix it with saliva in our mouths. When discussing the variety of foods that we eat, include discussion of special diets, including vegetarian diets.

Contents

About you

There are more than five billion human bodies on Earth. While we are all similar in many ways, we do have differences. What differences can you see between the children in the picture?

Can you think of any other animals that have body parts like ours?
How are these animals different from humans?

Work with a friend

Talk about the ways you and your friend are similar. Write down a list of your similarities.

Talk about the ways in which you are different. Record your differences.

Make sure you include these in your lists:

eye color
hair color
height
weight
waist measurement
foot length
hand size
arm length

Your skeleton

There are more than 200 bones in your body. Together they make up your skeleton.

Your skeleton protects important parts of your body. Your skull protects your brain. Your ribs protect your heart and lungs. Your skeleton also supports the soft parts of your body, such as the skin, and helps your body keep its shape.

 **Work with a friend**

Can you feel some bones through the skin?
Can you feel a kneecap?
How many bones can you feel in a leg?
How many bones can you feel in an arm?
Feel the skull. Where is the jaw bone?
How many ribs can you feel?
Can you feel the backbone?

On the move

Some part of your body is moving all the time. Your muscles make these movements possible. Muscles blink your eyes and move your tongue. You use muscles when you walk, run, jump, lift, and throw. Even when you are asleep, muscles are at work helping you to breathe. Look at the weightlifter's muscles in the picture.

Many bones in your body meet to form joints. Some joints, such as your knees and elbows, allow you to move around.

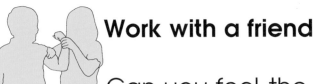

Work with a friend

Can you feel the muscle in your friend's upper arm?

Move your friend's forearm backward and forward. You can make this movement because the elbow has a hinge joint.

Find out more!

Where in your body can you find hinge joints?

Hands and feet

You use your hands every day to carry out many different jobs. Sometimes you use your hands to do delicate jobs, such as writing and painting. At other times you use them to do heavier jobs, such as lifting chairs.

Your feet help you to walk, jump, stand, and run. Both your hands and your feet contain bones, joints, and muscles. How are your hands and feet similar? Can you think of ways in which they are different?

When you run fast, your
muscles are working hard.
They need more oxygen,
so you breathe deeply
and quickly. Your heart
has to beat faster to
push the oxygen to
your muscles.

Place your hands
on your ribs.
Breathe in. Can
you feel your
rib cage get
bigger?
Inside your
ribs, your lungs
have gotten bigger
to take in air.
Breathe out.
Can you feel your rib
cage getting smaller?

Your amazing senses

Your senses allow you to hear, feel, see, taste, and smell things around you.

Your sense of touch tells you when something is hot, cold, rough, or smooth. You have touch sensors all over your skin. Your fingers are very sensitive. The children in the picture are holding a ball of ice. Can you guess how it feels?

Your tongue has sensors called taste buds so you can taste food and liquids.

Work with a friend

Try a taste test on one of your friends. Cut some food into small cubes. You could use apples, cheese, bananas, sugar cubes, carrots, lemons, onions, and potatoes.

Blindfold your friend. Let your friend taste each cube of food one at a time. Let your friend rinse his or her mouth with water before testing each new food. How many foods did your friend identify correctly?

⚠ Always use foods that you know are safe to eat. Ask an adult to help you cut up the food.

Find out more!

Can you think of a way to test your friend's sense of smell?

Looking at eyes

One way that you learn about the world is through your two eyes. The small black hole in the middle of your eye is called the pupil. It is here that light enters your eye. The light travels to a special part inside your eye called the retina. From the retina, signals are sent to your brain. Your brain sorts the signals into the images that you see.

Look at your eyes in a mirror.
Shine a flashlight on one eye.
Look at the size of the pupil.
Switch off the flashlight.
Wait a little while.
What happens to the size of the pupil?

Find out more!

Look at the color of the eyes of your friends. How could you find out which is the most common color? What is the least common eye color?

Ears to hear

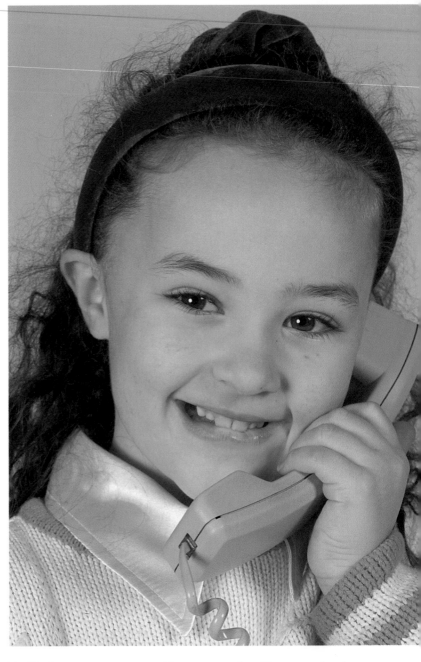

Sound travels as invisible waves through the air to your ears. These waves enter your ear and make a part of your ear called the eardrum vibrate. From the eardrum, sound messages are sent to your brain.

Sit quietly for a few minutes.
How many different sounds
can you hear?
Can you guess what the sounds
are made by?

Sprinkle some rice on top of a drum.
Hit the drum with a stick. Watch
how the drum vibrates and makes
the rice move. Your eardrum
vibrates when sounds hit it.

Find out more!

Hold a ruler over the edge of a table. "Twang" the free end to make it vibrate. How can you use your ruler to make high-pitched and low-pitched sounds?

Your skin and hair

Skin covers your whole body. It grows in layers. The top layer is dead skin. It flakes off and a new layer takes its place. Your skin protects all of your inner body parts from hits and bumps. It also prevents germs from entering your body.

Millions of hairs grow from your skin. These hairs help to keep you warm. Look at the skin on your arms with a magnifying glass. Are there any parts without hairs?

Hold a paper towel under some cold running water from a faucet. What happens to the towel? Now hold one of your hands under the running water. What do you notice?

You can see that your skin also protects your body from water.

Find out more!

Make fingerprints by pressing your fingertips on an ink pad and then pressing them on clean white paper. Roll each finger from side to side as you press down. Look at your prints with a magnifying glass. Do they all make the same pattern?

Your teeth

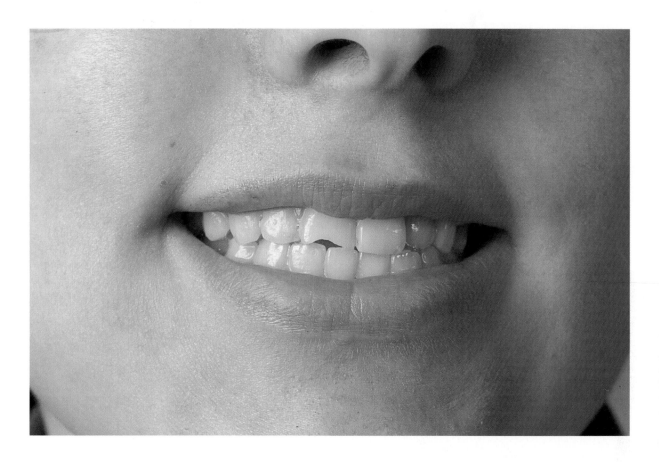

Your first teeth start to appear when you are about six months old. They are called your baby teeth. You may have 20 of these first teeth. They last a few years and then are replaced by new permanent teeth. An adult may have a full set of 32 teeth. Your front teeth are called incisors. They have sharp edges. Your back teeth are called molars. Feel the tops of your molars.

Use a mirror to look at your teeth. You can see that they are different shapes and sizes. The parts of your teeth not inside the gums are covered by a hard white material called enamel.

Find out how many teeth you have. Why is it important to clean your teeth every day?

Growing and staying healthy

You need food to help you grow and to give you energy. As food travels through your body, it is changed. We say it is "digested" by your body.

To stay healthy, your body needs a variety of foods, lots of exercise, and plenty of sleep every night.

Make a list of all the foods and liquids you have in three days. Have you eaten meat, fish, vegetables, and fresh fruit? These foods are good for you.

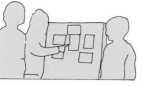

Work with some friends

Find a picture of yourself when you were a baby. Add more pictures to show how you looked on each birthday since then. Ask some friends to do the same. Talk to each other about how you have all changed.

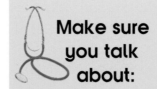

Make sure you talk about:

your height
your weight
your teeth
your skin
your voice
your hair
things that you can do

Index